RIGHTS & RESPONSIBILITIES

by

Grace Jones

CRABTREE
PUBLISHING COMPANY
WWW.CRABTREEBOOKS.COM

Published in Canada
Crabtree Publishing
616 Welland Avenue
St. Catharines, ON
L2M 5V6

Published in the United States
Crabtree Publishing
PMB 59051
350 Fifth Ave, 59th Floor
New York, NY 10118

Published in 2019 by Crabtree Publishing Company

First Published by Book Life in 2018
Copyright © 2018 Book Life

Author: Grace Jones

Editors: Kirsty Holmes, Janine Deschenes

Design: Daniel Scase

Proofreader: Ellen Rodger

Production coordinator and
  prepress technician (interior): Margaret Amy Salter

Prepress technician (covers): Ken Wright

Print coordinator: Katharine Berti

All facts, statistics, web addresses and URLs in this book were verified as valid and accurate at time of writing.
No responsibility for any changes to external websites or references can be accepted by either the author or publisher.

Photographs

Front Cover – arindambanerjee, Bennian. 2 – yuttana Contributor Studio. 4 – ra2studio, wavebreakmedia. 5 – Joseph Sohm. 6 – wavebreakmedia. 7 – neftali, Joseph Sohm. 8 – National Library of Ireland on The Commons. 9 – Kobby Dagan. 10 – Eric Buller Photography. 11 – TORWAISTUDIO. 12 – Eric Pasqualli. 13 – Osugi. 14 – Monkey Business Images, Iakov Filimonov. 15 – Rawpixel.com, Brian A Jackson. 16 – 7505811966, pryzmat. 17 – Rawpixel.com. 18 – Black Salmon. 19 – By SVRSLYIMAGE. 20 – Aipon. 21 – Drop of Light. 22 – MariaGershuni / Wikimedia Commons. 23 – By a katz. 24 – Diego G Diaz. 25 – Lucky Business, Blend Images. 26 – Sk Hasan Ali. 27 – Northfoto. 28 – © Claude Truong-Ngoc / Wikimedia Commons. 29 – coloursinmylife. 30 – Monkey Business Images.

Printed in the U.S.A./082018/CG20180601

Library and Archives Canada Cataloguing in Publication

Jones, Grace, 1990-, author
        Rights and responsibilities / Grace Jones.

(Our values)
Includes index.
Issued in print and electronic formats.
ISBN 978-0-7787-5191-5 (hardcover).--
ISBN 978-0-7787-5202-8 (softcover).--
ISBN 978-1-4271-2141-7 (HTML)

        1. Political participation--Juvenile literature. 2. Civil rights--Juvenile literature. I. Title.

JF799.J66 2018   j323'.042   C2018-902422-4
                                           C2018-902423-2

Library of Congress Cataloging-in-Publication Data

Names: Jones, Grace, 1990- author.
Title: Rights and responsibilities / Grace Jones.
Description: New York, New York : Crabtree Publishing, 2019. |
  Series: Our values | Includes index.
Identifiers: LCCN 2018021340 (print) | LCCN 2018029277 (ebook) |
  ISBN 9781427121417 (Electronic) |
  ISBN 9780778751915(hardcover) |
  ISBN 9780778752028(paperback)
Subjects: LCSH: Civil rights--Juvenile literature. | Human rights--Juvenile
  literature. | Civil rights. sears | Human rights. sears |
  Responsibility. sears
Classification: LCC JC571 (ebook) | LCC JC571 .J585 2019 (print) |
  DDC 323--dc23
LC record available at https://lccn.loc.gov/2018021340

CONTENTS

Words that are **boldfaced** can be found in the glossary on page 31.

WHAT ARE RIGHTS?

What makes you free to express yourself, pursue your interests, vote, follow your beliefs, or be treated fairly by others? You have rights! Rights are the freedoms you have to do all of the things above, and more. If someone has the **authority** or permission to do something, we say it is their right to do it. Often, our rights are protected by **laws**. This means that our freedom to do something is **upheld** by the government. No one can legally stop us from exercising, or using, that right. Rights protected by laws are called legal rights. But there are other kinds of rights, too. And all of your rights come with responsibilities—especially the responsibility to make sure everyone's rights are upheld.

The Bill of Rights in the United States, and the Charter of Rights and Freedoms in Canada, are documents that tell citizens the rights they have under the laws of each country. Can you search online to find the document that explains the legal rights in your country?

HUMAN RIGHTS

Some rights, called human rights, that are considered to be universal because they belong to all people, just because they are human. Human rights help people live with freedom, **equality**, **justice** and peace. After World War II, the United Nations created the Universal Declaration of Human Rights (UDHR). This is a list of human rights that the United Nations says all countries should uphold for their citizens. The UDHR includes the right to:

- **Liberty**
- Security, or safety
- **Be free from slavery**
- Be free from cruel punishment
- **A fair trial**
- Move freely within and outside their country

The right to vote is a legal right, because most governments create laws granting their citizens the right to vote, but it is also considered a human right by the UDHR.

Sometimes, people disagree about what is a human right and what isn't. Who you are or where you live in the world can change your point of view on what you believe to be a human right. In some countries or areas on Earth, the rights in the UDHR are **violated**. People there may not have access to the basic rights to freedom of speech, religion, equality, and liberty. Rights violations can happen because of war or conflict in an area.

They can also happen if a government leader in a country forces the people who live there to live or think a certain way. In Iran, anyone who speaks out against the government is punished. Women there do not have the right to equality. They must wear head coverings called hijabs, and are not allowed to do some of the same things as men, such as watch sports in stadiums. Some brave women there are speaking out against the violation of their rights.

LEGAL RIGHTS

Legal rights are rights that are recognized and **enforced** by the law in a country. If there is a violation of a legal right, it is punished by the law. Courts of law enforce legal rights. Legal rights are usually connected with human rights. They state the basic rights that people in a country have as citizens, or because they live there. They are equally available to most people in most countries without **discrimination**.

THE RIGHT TO A FAIR TRIAL IS A LEGAL RIGHT AS WELL AS A HUMAN RIGHT. THIS RIGHT MEANS THAT PEOPLE WHO ARE CHARGED WITH A CRIME CAN FAIRLY DEFEND THEMSELVES IN **COURT**.

People's legal rights can change from country to country because governments in different countries create different laws. For example, the right for same-sex couples to marry is a legal right in many countries, such as Canada, the United States, South Africa, and Australia. But this legal right is not upheld in every country. Countries such as Sudan ban same-sex marriage and relationships.

Other countries violate the human rights of their citizens if they are found to be in a same-sex relationship. In Sudan, people are punished and sometimes killed if they are found to be in a same-sex relationship. In those countries, the laws are usually related to religious beliefs that say same-sex relationships are wrong.

CIVIL RIGHTS

Civil rights are those rights which provide each person equal opportunities and equal protection of their legal rights. Civil rights are similar to human rights, such as the right to life, liberty, and equality. However, unlike human rights, civil rights are granted and upheld by governments. Examples of civil rights include freedom of speech and the right to vote. Important civil rights movements of the past have made sure that all people have equal opportunities. Nelson Mandela fought against **apartheid** in South Africa, which **segregated** citizens based on their race or the color of their skin. In the United States, civil rights activists in the 1950s and 60s helped abolish segregation laws. Segregation violates civil rights.

IN 1955, ROSA PARKS PROTESTED SEGREGATION BY REFUSING TO GIVE HER BUS SEAT TO A WHITE PASSENGER. SHE IS SOMETIMES CALLED THE "MOTHER OF THE CIVIL RIGHTS MOVEMENT" BECAUSE HER ACTIONS BEGAN A WAVE OF PROTESTS.

POLITICAL RIGHTS

Every person has the right to share in how their country is being run. This can include having the right to vote in fair elections, to oppose or criticize the government, to organize or join political groups, and even to be elected to **public office**. These are all political rights and they are guaranteed to people who live in **democracies**. But there here are many countries around the world where people do not have political rights. In non-democratic countries, such as North Korea, people do not have a say in who leads them. This is an example of political rights being violated.

7

ECONOMIC, SOCIAL, AND CULTURAL RIGHTS

Economic rights, social rights, and cultural rights are often mentioned together. Each of these rights help ensure a person has an equal opportunity to function and succeed in society. These rights allow people to enjoy a good standard of living. This means that their basic needs are met. Economic, social, and cultural rights are also meant to make sure a person's standard of living is adequate for their health and well-being. These rights ensure that a person can act as a contributing member of their community and practice their culture. According to the United Nations, economic, social, and cultural rights are **fundamental** rights for everyone, and governments should make and abide by laws that protect these rights.

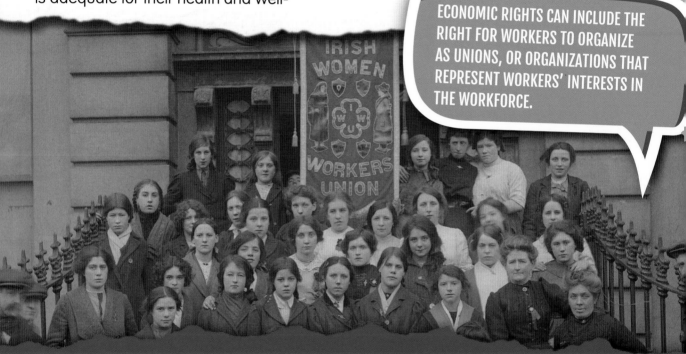

ECONOMIC RIGHTS CAN INCLUDE THE RIGHT FOR WORKERS TO ORGANIZE AS UNIONS, OR ORGANIZATIONS THAT REPRESENT WORKERS' INTERESTS IN THE WORKFORCE.

ECONOMIC RIGHTS

Economic rights provide people with the financial security they need to support themselves and their families. Economic rights include the right to safe employment without **discrimination.** Economic rights also include the right to basic support from the state when people cannot work because of illness, injury, or a disability. These rights ensure that people are able to earn money and access services that allow them to live. Worker's rights are economic rights. These include the right to safe work and to be paid fairly for their labor. Many democratic countries protect these rights. Some pass laws with even greater protections.

SOCIAL RIGHTS

Social rights are those that allow a person an equal opportunity to function and succeed in their community. They can include the right to education, so that a person can go to school to receive the skills they need to work and learn about the world. They can include the right to physical and mental health, and the right to health care and assistance. These rights mean that a person has a right to be healthy and receive care. Social rights can also include the right to housing. A person cannot be forcibly evicted, or made homeless. Their home needs to be a safe place to live. The rights to safe, clean water to drink and healthy food to eat are also social rights. If the water supply in a city is **contaminated**, the rights of the people who live there are being violated. In every country, these human rights must be backed by laws.

CULTURAL RIGHTS MAKE SURE THAT CULTURAL DIVERSITY IS RESPECTED AND HONORED IN SOCIETY. ONE WAY TO HONOR CULTURE IS TO ATTEND CULTURAL FESTIVALS.

CULTURAL RIGHTS

Cultural rights allow a person to practice their culture or participate in culture in the place where they live. This means that they can access and appreciate cultural heritage—whether that be by visiting museums, attending cultural festivities, or organizing cultural events. Cultural rights also ensure that a person is allowed to speak in their language of choice, eat the food of their choosing, and create art. This means that the speaking of non-dominant languages cannot be banned. Culture allows people to express themselves, connect positively with others, and feel proud of their identity.

CHILDREN'S RIGHTS

All people have the same human rights. But in most countries, children, also called minors, do not have the same legal rights as adults. They may also have different civic and political rights. In most countries, children aren't legally considered to be adults until the age of 18. Due to the fact that their brains are still developing, they are not considered to have the same decision-making ability that adults do. Usually, minors cannot vote or run for office. In many countries, they are also punished under different laws if they commit a crime. There are also different laws about a minor's right to work or to **consent** to marriage or sexual activity. These laws were created to protect children and youth.

IN COUNTRIES SUCH AS PAPUA NEW GUINEA, YEMEN, AND LIBERIA THERE ARE NO LAWS THAT DEFINE WHEN A PERSON BECOMES AN ADULT.

The age at which a minor is considered an adult, often called the age of majority, changes from country to country—and sometimes from region to region within a country. The examples below show the differences around the world.

- United States: 18 or 19, depending on the state
- Canada: 18 or 19, depending on the province
- Singapore: 21 years old
- South Korea and Algeria: 19 years old
- Iran: 15 years old for males and 9 years old for females
- Saudi Arabia: 15 years old

Usually, parents or a guardian look after and make decisions for a child so they are protected. Most countries also have some laws that specifically protect children from harm. In most countries, children have the right to a safe environment and for their basic needs to be provided by their parents or guardians.

If a country's authorities assess that a child is unsafe in their home or not being adequately cared for, they usually have the power to remove that child from their home for their protection. The child may be placed in foster care or returned home if it becomes a safer place to live.

IN MOST COUNTRIES, THE MINIMUM WORKING AGE IS AROUND 14 TO 16 YEARS OLD, BUT IN SYRIA, PARAGUAY AND BANGLADESH, THE MINIMUM WORKING AGE IS JUST 12 YEARS OLD.

CHILD LABOR

In many countries, children have the right to an education and are protected by laws against working before they reach a certain age—usually from 14 to 16 years old. Some laws also limit the number of hours minors can work. But in some areas of the world, children have little or no access to education and, instead, must work long hours or are forced to serve as soldiers.

Sometimes, children living in **poverty** must work to help support their families. In some countries, children are **exploited** for child labor or for military service, because they are a **vulnerable** group who cannot fight back. Children who are exploited in this way can often work in very harsh conditions, sometimes without food or water, for very long hours.

CHILD MARRIAGE

Laws that limit marriage to consenting adults also protect children from being exploited. These laws usually say that a person cannot get married until they are 18 years old, or until they are no longer considered a minor. But some countries with these laws also say that a minor can get married at age 16 with parental consent. In some American states, even younger minors can get married with the permission of a judge.

However, many rights organizations believe that these exceptions should not be allowed because they take away the minor's right to choose—leaving the decision up to parents or the judicial system. This could be a violation of their right to protection by adults. In some countries, there is no minimum age for marriage. For example, in Niger, Mozambique, and Mali, over 50 percent of girls are married before 18.

NIGER HAD THE HIGHEST RATE OF CHILD MARRIAGE IN 2017, WITH 76 PERCENT OF GIRLS BEING MARRIED BEFORE AGE 18.

THE FACTS

According to the organization Human Rights Watch, 15 million girls younger than age 18 marry each year.

• In Yemen, 64 percent of girls are married before the age of 18.
• Almost two in five girls in Tanzania are married before the age of 18.
• In Bangladesh, 81 percent of girls are married before the age of 18.
• Close to 250,000 girls from 12 to 18 years old were married in the United States between 2000 and 2010.

THE UN CONVENTION ON THE RIGHTS OF THE CHILD

The United Nations (UN) is a world organization that is responsible for maintaining international peace and security throughout the world. In 1989, the UN created a treaty called the Convention on the Rights of the Child to protect the political, economic, social, health, and cultural rights of people under the age of 18.

PICTURED HERE IS THE UN HEADQUARTERS IN NEW YORK CITY.

193 countries are part of the United Nations, and they are required to follow the conditions that are set out in the treaty under international law. The treaty protects children's rights throughout the world. Some of the conditions are:

- Respect the rights of each child without discrimination against race, sex, language, religion, or disability.
- In all actions concerning children, the best interests of the child should be put first.
- Parents or guardians are responsible for the survival and development of a child to the maximum extent possible.
- Children should have the right to freedom of expression at all times.

WHY ARE RIGHTS IMPORTANT?

There are different ways of classifying, or organizing, the types of rights, but all rights are fundamentally similar—they allow people to live freely and give them an equal opportunity to enjoy a good standard of living. Rights are important because they protect the minimum standards necessary for people to live with respect and dignity. Human rights give people the freedom to choose how they live and the liberty to express themselves. Human rights are also able to protect people because they are able to limit the amount of power a government can have over their citizens. This helps stop governments from influencing or trying to control its citizens' choices and beliefs.

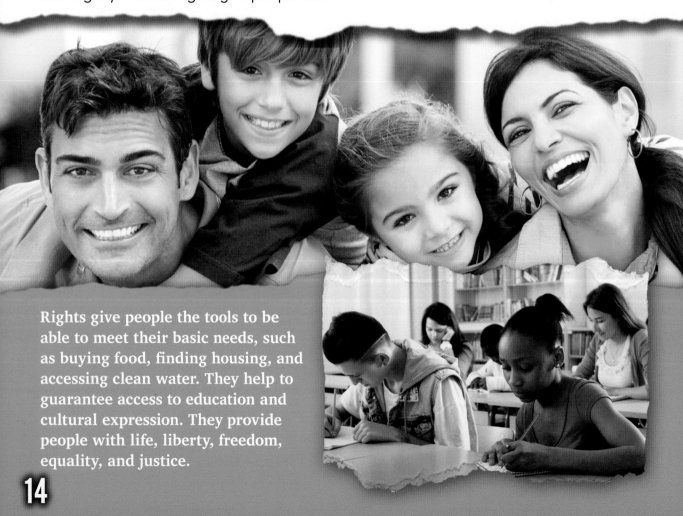

Rights give people the tools to be able to meet their basic needs, such as buying food, finding housing, and accessing clean water. They help to guarantee access to education and cultural expression. They provide people with life, liberty, freedom, equality, and justice.

Human rights are universal and **internationally guaranteed**. This means that some of the most important organizations in the world, such as the UN, Human Rights Watch, and governments from some of the world's most powerful countries, have agreed to protect the human rights of every person on the planet. Unfortunately, the international guarantee of human rights is not always upheld.

HUMAN RIGHTS WATCH IS AN ORGANIZATION THAT WORKS WITH HUMAN RIGHTS AND TRIES TO PROTECT THEM ALL AROUND THE WORLD.

HUMAN RIGHTS

RIGHTS
POWER
FAIRNESS
FREEDOM

MANY COUNTRIES AROUND THE WORLD DO NOT PROTECT THE RIGHTS OF THEIR CITIZENS.

While rights are designed to protect people, the rights themselves also need to be protected so that they aren't taken away. It can be difficult for a person to protect their own rights, especially if rights are being taken away or denied by governments or other people in power. That is why many organizations have dedicated themselves to protecting the rights of people all over the world. Unfortunately, the governments in some countries do not like or allow these organizations to protect the human rights of the people who live there.

WHAT ARE RESPONSIBILITIES?

A responsibility is a duty which people accept they should do or fulfill. You have just read about the rights you have as a human being and as a citizen of your country. All of your rights come with responsibilities. People have the responsibility to act in ways that uphold and protect our own rights and the rights of people around us. We also have the responsibility to act in ways that create a positive local and global community.

Every citizen has responsibilities towards the country in which they live. Citizens of a country are responsible to support and defend their rights and the rights of other citizens. They are responsible to show respect toward other citizens. They are also responsible to follow the laws in their country and to participate in **elections** as voters. Voting is a right and a responsibility. The right to vote means you have the right to have a say in who runs your country. But you are responsible to uphold this right for yourself by making sure you vote in elections.

RESPONSIBILITIES IN YOUR COMMUNITY

A community is a place where people live, work, and play. It includes your home, school, neighborhood, and any places you go to pursue your interests or interact with others. You have the right to have your basic needs, such as your need for food and shelter, met in your community. You also have the right to participate in your community.

However, you are responsible to uphold those rights for yourself and others. For example, you have the right to participate in cultural activities in your community. This means you have the responsibility to go out in your community and learn about the different cultures that exist there!

Your responsibility to uphold the rights of others in your community affects all of the people who live there. You also depend on others to fulfill their responsibility to uphold your rights. Some of the responsibilities you have in your community are:

- Keeping your community a clean and healthy place to live by treating the physical environment with respect. Avoid contributing to pollution, make an effort to reduce the amount of waste you create, and do not litter.
- Taking part in community life by getting involved in clubs and events.
- Helping to make sure others' basic needs are met by volunteering or raising money for local community projects and charities.
- Speaking to others in your community. The best way to understand the place that you live in is through speaking with others. Learn about their cultures and backgrounds, and support their right to express themselves.

PROTECTING RIGHTS IN YOUR COMMUNITY

As a member of your community and a citizen of your country, you also have the responsibility to help protect the rights of others. You can do this by volunteering or donating to charities that work to ensure people's basic human rights are met. You can also speak out when you see that others' rights are being violated.

People speak out by participating in protests or **demonstrations**, writing to their local politician to ask for changes in laws, and even by posting their ideas online using blogs or **vlogs**. Remember that you have the right to express yourself—and you have the responsibility to speak up for rights in your community.

Organizing a drive to donate clothing to those in need is one way that youth can help uphold the basic rights of others in their community.

RESPONSIBILITIES AT SCHOOL

You have the right to an education. But you also have a responsibility to participate in your learning and make your school a safe, welcoming place for everyone. Some of your responsibilities at school include:

- **Treating everyone with respect. Listen when others are talking, respect their opinions, and remember that everyone has the right to express themselves. Being respectful helps everyone feel safe and welcome at school.**
- Following the rules that the school have set at all times. Rules are made to keep you and other students safe.
- **Looking after school property and not damaging things. Your right to education depends on having a clean, safe school and tools with which to learn.**

RESPONSIBILITIES AT HOME

According to your human rights and economic, social, and cultural rights, you have the right to a safe home in which to live. But with your rights come responsibilities! You have the responsibility to make your home a safe place to live. You can make sure your house is physically safe by helping to keep it clean and **accessible** for the people who live there. You can also help keep your house safe by respecting the people who live there. To respect someone means to take into account their feelings and needs.

You can show respect to others at home by upholding their right to freedom of speech. Remember that even if you don't agree with a family member, you both have the right to express yourselves!

RESPONSIBILITIES AT WORK

You may not be working yet, but it is also important to uphold workers' rights. At a workplace, employees can help to make sure that people have the right to a safe place of work that is free from discrimination. Employees also have the responsibility to respect their coworkers and follow the rules at work. Responsibilities at work can include:

- Following rules such as arriving to work on time, meeting deadlines and goals, and being reliable. This means coworkers can depend on each other.
- **Treating coworkers with kindness and respect. This helps make a workplace a safe and welcoming place for all people.**
- Learning about the rights that you have as a worker and supporting those rights for all coworkers.

GLOBAL RESPONSIBILITIES

All of the people on Earth are part of a global community. We all share the planet on which we live. That means that in addition to being citizens of the countries in which we live, and members of the local communities in which we live and go to school, we are **global citizens**. As global citizens, we have the responsibility to uphold the human rights of all people on Earth.

We are all part of one big, global community and with that comes many responsibilities. They can include:

ONE RESPONSIBILITY GLOBAL CITIZENS HAVE IS TO RESPECT AND SUPPORT OTHER PEOPLES' RIGHT TO FREELY PRACTICE A RELIGION.

- **Understanding and respecting other people's perspectives, even if they are different to our own.**
- Learning about rights violations around the world and supporting efforts to uphold human rights for all people.
- **Building relationships with people from other countries and cultures to understand different perspectives.**

YOU ARE A GLOBAL CITIZEN

Just as a citizen of a country has certain responsibilities in the country in which they live, you have responsibilities on Earth as a global citizen. It's important to see yourself as part of a community in which all of the other people on Earth depend on you. Your choice to be responsible for upholding human rights for all people matters, and makes a difference. When everyone in the global community takes on the responsibility to uphold human rights, we can help to create a world in which all people can thrive and be successful. By taking responsibility, you make the world a better place.

If someone is the leader of a government, they are responsible for the whole country that they represent and govern. They are also responsible for working with other leaders to make sure people's rights are upheld all over the world.

GLOBAL LEADERS WHO ARE PART OF NATO, A MILITARY ALLIANCE BETWEEN 29 COUNTRIES, MEET EVERY TWO YEARS.

There are many ways that you can take responsibility for upholding the human rights of people around the world. Learn about the basic rights that all people are entitled to. Research where those rights are respected, as well as where they are being violated. Are all people on Earth free from harm and able to fulfill their basic needs? When you learn about human rights violations, speak out against them. Tell other people what you learned. Create a blog or vlog post about what you learned online. Write a letter to your government asking them to support efforts to uphold the human rights of all people. Learn about and support organizations that are helping to ensure all people have their rights respected and protected.

PROTECTING RIGHTS
AROUND THE WORLD

People all around the world are taking steps to protect human rights on Earth and make the world a better place. The Global Goals for **Sustainable** Development are a list of 17 goals that are meant to improve life on Earth. They were signed by global leaders in 2015, who agreed to try and meet these goals by 2030. Many of the global goals relate to making sure that human rights are upheld for all people on Earth. The goals include:

- **Ending poverty and hunger**
- Making sure all people have access to clean water
- **Providing all people with quality education**
- Ensuring all people can enjoy good health and well-being
- **Achieving gender equality and supporting the success of women and girls**
- Reducing inequalities in society and ensuring that opportunities for success are available to all people, regardless of their gender, race, economic status, or other differences
- **Promoting decent work for all by protecting labor rights and ending slavery**

Global leaders agreed to these goals. But as global citizens, we also have the responsibility to support these goals and make changes guided by them. Visit www.globalgoals.org to view the goals and to learn more about this initiative. How can you uphold your responsibility as a global citizen to help support these goals and make the world a place in which all people's rights are supported?

PROTECTING EARTH

We also have the responsibility to make sure that Earth is a safe place to live—for all living things. We share Earth with millions of **species** of plants and animals. It is our responsibility to protect the planet that we all depend on. The global goals uphold this responsibility by tackling **climate change**, supporting plant and animal life on land and beneath water, generating clean energy, and creating sustainable cities and communities. Each of these goals works to protect Earth and its living things.

In April 2016, global leaders met to sign the Paris Agreement. To meet the agreement's goals, many countries need to work together.

Mission 2020 is a global goal that sparked from the Paris Agreement and the Global Goals for Sustainable Development. It is a strategy to rapidly decrease global greenhouse gas emissions, which contribute to global warming, by 2020.

The Paris Agreement, signed by 195 countries, is a global action plan meant to fight global warming. Mission 2020 requires countries to take responsibility for the emissions they create, and take steps to protect Earth by reducing those emissions significantly by 2020. This is meant to make sure the global temperature does not rise too much. It is one way that countries around the world are working together to uphold their responsibility to protect Earth.

WHY ARE RESPONSIBILITIES IMPORTANT?

Responsibilities are important because they can help to protect people's rights. It's vital to remember that rights and responsibilities are linked. With every right comes a responsibility to uphold and protect that right. For example, everyone has the right to practice any religion that they choose, but we also have the responsibility to respect people who practice different religions and support their right to do so.

WHEN THE MEMBERS OF THE STANDING ROCK SIOUX RESERVATION PROTESTED FOR THEIR RIGHT TO CLEAN WATER, MANY OTHER CITIZENS TRAVELED THERE TO SUPPORT THEIR CAUSE.

Sometimes, we can take our rights for granted. For example, if you live in a democracy, you might take your right to vote for granted. But it is important to remember that many of our rights were once fought for by people in the past. In the early 1900s, women fought for their right to vote. In the 1950s and 1960s, African-Americans such as Rosa Parks fought for their right to equality by ending segregation. People around the world—and even people in your own country—are still fighting for their right to vote, their right to freedom, their right to free speech, and more. Rights are only upheld when people take up their responsibility to fight for them. We cannot take our rights for granted.

BEING ACCOUNTABLE

Knowing our responsibilities holds us accountable for ourselves and for all people on Earth. To be accountable means to take ownership of our actions. It means that we understand how our actions affect others, and know that we can make a difference in our local and global communities.

Make a list of choices you can make that support the rights of people in your local and global communities.

Some clothing companies use child labor or employ workers in factories where they are not safe. One way you can be accountable is to buy clothing from companies that uphold the rights of their workers.

Responsibilities are important because they help us see how all people are connected. All people on Earth are deserving of human rights and we depend on one another to protect our rights. Learning about our responsibilities to uphold rights means that we can make choices that will support the rights of others. The world becomes a better place when we realize that we are all responsible for upholding the rights of all people.

UPHOLDING OUR RIGHTS AND RESPONSIBILITIES

Now more than ever, human rights are becoming better protected. Most countries are now governed by democratic governments and their citizens have political and civil rights. Between 1950 and today, the number of people living in democracies has increased from 793 million to 3.8 billion. However, much still needs to be done to protect the rights of all people—even in democratic countries.

Rohingya refugees are often turned away by other countries. When this happens, their right to a safe home is being violated.

Around half of the world's population still does not have access to some civic, political, economic, social, cultural, or human rights. North Korea is an example of one country where citizens live under a dictatorship, which is a system where one person holds all power over a country's citizens. In North Korea, there is no freedom of speech or religion. Other basic rights are violated there too, such as the right to freedom. Many people are imprisoned or punished there if they disagree with the government. In some countries, poverty, war, and other conflict have violated even the most basic human rights—to life and to freedom. In Myanmar, the **Rohingya** people have faced decades of discrimination and violence because of their **ethnicity**. They are a stateless population, which means that Myanmar does not recognize their citizenship. This limits their freedom of movement and right to access basic services, such as health care. Since 2017, the Rohingya are being killed and forced from their homes as a part of an **ethnic cleansing** campaign by the country's government. Their basic right to life is being violated and threatened every day.

WORKING TOGETHER

If we want to protect rights better in the future, countries need to work together. International organizations such as the United Nations, which involves nearly all countries in the world, encourage collaboration between countries to uphold the human rights of all people on Earth. Many people rely on the **humanitarian** aid that the United Nations provides. The United Nations Children's Fund (UNICEF) provides children's aid. The United Nations Refugee Agency (UNHCR) provides aid to refugees. The UN also has soldiers known as Blue Helmets, who work to promote peace in areas of conflict and protect people against violence.

THE UN'S BLUE HELMET SOLDIERS TRY TO UPHOLD THE HUMAN RIGHTS TO LIFE, FREEDOM, AND SAFETY AROUND THE WORLD.

The United Nations is not the only international organization that works to uphold human rights around the world. International non-governmental organizations (NGOs) such as Amnesty International, the International Red Cross, and CARE work to uphold the basic human rights of all people by providing humanitarian aid during crises. In Syria, The White Helmets are an organization that works to protect citizens from civil war violence. You can be a responsible global citizen by learning about the different aid organizations working to protect human rights around the world.

YOUTH WHO FIGHT FOR RIGHTS

As global citizens, we have the responsibility to make sure people's rights around the world are upheld. In many countries, youth are fighting for their rights to education, safety, democracy, and more. Their stories inspire others around the world to uphold the rights of all people. The Taliban is a terrorist organization that follows a strict **interpretation** of religion of Islam. It does not believe women and men have equal rights. When the Taliban took control of the Swat Valley in Pakistan in 2007, they stopped girls and women from going to school, voting, and working, and also banned watching television, dancing, and listening to music. Many schools for girls were closed. One female student, Malala Yousafzai, began to write anonymously for a blog, telling the world about the Taliban's unfair laws.

PICTURED HERE AT THE AWARD CEREMONY, MALALA YOUSAFZAI WAS THE YOUNGEST PERSON TO RECEIVE THE NOBEL PEACE PRIZE IN 2014.

After the Taliban found out Malala was the person behind the blog, they started to send her family death threats. One day in 2012, fifteen-year-old Malala was shot by a member of the Taliban. She was rushed to the hospital in critical condition, but made a miraculous recovery. Malala continues to advocate for girls' rights to education. Her refusal to be silenced has brought hope to millions of people around the world who don't have access to education or whose rights are being threatened.

Joshua Wong is a pro-democracy activist in Hong Kong, a **territory** of China since 1997. He and other students there felt that China was controlling too much about life in Hong Kong, such as what is taught in schools and how the government is elected and run. At age fifteen, Joshua co-founded a group called Scholarism. He and the group fight for the right for Hong Kong citizens to vote for their own government. Joshua has faced intense opposition from the Chinese government and its supporters. He was jailed twice—once in 2017 and once in 2018— for participating in protests. Despite this, Joshua continues to fight for democracy in Hong Kong and has drawn international support for his cause.

JOSHUA HELPED GATHER SUPPORT FOR DEMOCRACY IN HONG KONG BY ORGANIZING AND SPEAKING AT DEMONSTRATIONS, SUCH AS THIS ONE IN 2015.

Malala and Joshua are two of many youth activists fighting for their rights around the world. Payal Jangid fights for children's rights in India, speaking out against child marriage and labor there. Like Malala, Payal believes that all children have a right to education, and has received international recognition. In Florida, survivors of the February 2018 shooting at Marjory Stoneman Douglas High School started the Never Again movement to fight for their right to safety and protection at school. They organized protests for stricter gun control and inspired other school students around the United States to stand up for their right to safety at school too.

THINK ABOUT IT

1 What is a right? What is a responsibility? How are these things related, and why are they important in our local and global communities?

2 Review the stories of youth who fight for rights on pages 28 and 29. Discuss how each of these youth upholds their responsibilities as global citizens and members of their communities.

3 Look up the Universal Declaration of Human Rights and the UN Convention on the Rights of the Child. In what way can you help uphold those rights for all people on Earth?

GLOSSARY

accessible	Describes a place that is easily reached or entered
apartheid	A government-controlled system in South Africa from 1948 until 1991 that separated nonwhite and white citizens—and allowed for discrimination and marginalization of nonwhite citizens
authority	the power to give orders or make decisions
climate change	A change in the usual weather and temperature on Earth—usually referring to the warming of Earth's temperature due to human activity
consent	To give permission
contaminated	Polluted by outside substances
court	The place where lawyers, juries, and judges meet to decide court cases
democracies	governments that have been elected fairly
demonstrations	A public meeting protesting or expressive views on an issue
discrimination	the action of treating people unjustly for reasons such as their race, gender, and age
election	An organized process in which citizens vote to choose their government
enforced	to put or keep in place by force
equality	the state of being equal, especially in rights, status, and opportunity
ethnic cleansing	The organized, mass murder of a population based on their ethnicity
ethnicity	A person's shared background of cultural traditions
exploited	to have used a person or situation in an unfair way
fair trial	A way to justly determine who is innocent and guilty
fundamental	Essential or of central importance
global citizen	Someone who is part of the global community of all people on Earth
humanitarian aid	Assistance provided to people in dire need—usually meant to save lives or end suffering
internationally guaranteed	Promised by countries around the world to make sure that a duty is met
interpretation	Explaining the meaning of something
justice	That which is right and fair
laws	A system of rules that people in a country follow
legal representation	Lawyers who defend a person in court
liberty	The state of being free
poverty	Being extremely poor; struggling to meet basic needs
public office	A position of authority to represent people in a community, especially in government
Rohingya	An ethnic group of Muslim people who live in Rakhine State in western Myanmar
segregated	The act of separating or setting apart people into groups
species	A type or class of living thing such as an animal or insect
sustainable	Describes actions that have a low impact on the environment
territory	An area that is under the control of another country or ruler
upheld	To protect and support
violated	Failing to respect someone's rights
vlogs	A blog in which someone shares their thoughts in video form
vulnerable	At risk

INDEX